The true cost of terrorism: lost civil liberties

By Roger A. Donaldson, II

December 2015

This paper was written to describe the civil liberties that United States citizens traded in an effort to feel safe after the terror attacks on 9/11.

Abstract

The purpose of this paper is to explore the rights that were established by the founding fathers through the constitution and the effects that the fear of terrorism has had on those rights. The ideologies of the writers of the Constitution and subsequent amendments are explored, as well as the state of the nation when these documents were made into law. The major terrorist attack at the World Trade Center sparked a multitude of legislation and with that legislation new offices and reorganized offices were formed and challenged with the task of protecting the citizens of the United States. With this "protection" came consequences, however, as many rights given in the Constitution are now suppressed, and the United States government basically has a green light to do as it pleases, as long as they say their actions are to prevent terrorism.

Introduction:

After the terrorist attacks on the World Trade Center in September of 2001, there has been much debate on the loss of personal freedoms as guaranteed in the Constitution and the Bill of Rights. Americans were outraged, and the war on terrorism was used to suppress individual rights and further agendas of some unscrupulous politicians. Many new law-enforcement and intelligence agencies were formed and budgets were increased of existing agencies. It is important to look back through the history of the constitution and its application however, as one will find that shortly after inception rights were suppressed to supposedly guarantee national security and to safeguard the population. The writers of the Constitution were still in office when the first suppression of rights came about. President Lincoln, who many feel is one of America's greatest presidents, ignored the Bill of Rights and stopped the publishing of anti-war sentiment and locked up many citizens without trial or due process. There is a balance between national security and individual rights that must be maintained. The real question is whether suppression of rights is really necessary and effective at preventing terrorism.

Chapter 1

The Constitution and Bill of Rights

The Constitution of the United States is the document that was created by the Founding Fathers of the country to establish specific roles, rights, and responsibilities of the federal government and the citizens of the United States. This document that outlines the system of federal government for the United States was drawn up at the Constitutional Convention in Philadelphia in 1787 to replace the original charter of the United States, the Articles of Confederation, which was deemed inadequate. Deemed a living document, the Constitution of the United States is very concise, and its general statement of principles was designed to make possible the extension of meanings to foster the continuous growth of the country. One of the ways that the Constitution of the United States is able to remain valid after some 200 years is that the wording is very general. Interpretation from the judicial branch is needed from time to time to determine what exactly is meant and what is "constitutional". This makes for some controversy as some people believe in a strict interpretation, and some believe in a loose interpretation. Since the inception of the Constitution of the United States, 27 amendments have been adopted. Most of the amendments to the constitution were brought on by Supreme Court decisions, but the first ten amendments, called the Bill of Rights, were added within two years of the signing of the federal Constitution to ensure sufficient guarantees of individual liberties. ("Constitution of," 2013)

The Bill of Rights was written by James Madison in response to calls from several states for greater constitutional protection for individual liberties. The Bill of Rights lists specific prohibitions on governmental power. The Virginia Declaration of Rights strongly influenced Madison. One of the many debates between Federalists and Anti-Federalists was the Constitution's lack of a bill of rights that would place specific limits on government power. Federalists argued that the Constitution did not need a bill of rights, because the people and the states kept any powers not given to the federal government. Anti-Federalists held that a bill of rights was necessary to safeguard individual liberty. Madison, a member of the U.S. House of Representatives, went through the Constitution, making changes where he thought most appropriate. But, several Representatives led by Roger Sherman objected by saying that Congress had no authority to change the wording of the Constitution itself; it was agreed to present Madison's changes as a list of 17 amendments. However, when passed to the Senate only 12 amendments survived. When sent to the states for ratification, only ten were adopted. These ten became the Bill of Rights, which is basically a list of limits on government power. For example, what the Founders saw as the natural right of individuals to speak and worship freely was protected by the First Amendment's prohibitions on Congress from making laws establishing a religion or suppressing freedom of speech. The natural right of being free from the government in one's own home was safeguarded by the Fourth Amendment's warrant requirements. ("Bill of Rights")

The First, Fourth, and Fifth amendments are under the most scrutiny as of late when it comes to current events in the United States. The First Amendment to the United States Constitution guarantees the freedom of worship, of speech, of press, of assembly, and of petition to the government for redress of grievances. ("Constitution of," 2013) The founders of the Constitution, including George Washington, James Madison, Alexander Hamilton, and Rufus King, were known to support non-citizens in the right to petition. The first private bill in United States history responded to a non-citizens petition. This history is consistent with the English and Colonial right of petition extending to all persons irrespective of citizenship. ("The meaning," 2013) The Fourth Amendment to the United States Constitution protects against unreasonable search and seizure. ("Constitution of," 2013) This amendment emerged from several premises of the Colonial era. One premise being that "A man's home is his castle." Another being that law enforcement officials cannot obtain "general warrants." James Madison, the amendment's original drafter, examined various proposals and rejected one that would have limited protection to only the "citizens." *("The meaning," 2013)* The Fifth Amendment states that no person shall be held for "a capital or otherwise infamous crime" without indictment, be tried twice for the same offense, be compelled to testify against oneself, or "be deprived of life, liberty, or property without due process of law." The phrase "due process of law" is also used in the Fourteenth Amendment. ("Constitution of," 2013) James Madison's political ideology was that man had several fundamental rights that needed to be guaranteed to him. Religious liberty, freedom of speech, and due process guaranteed against an unsupported governmental authority. Madison and his supporters were passionate about these rights and were quick to speak out against and change the law when the Alien and Sedition Act was passed by authoring the Virginia Compromise in 1789, which declared the Alien and Sedition Act unconstitutional. ("Miller Center")

Almost a century later and after the most trying event in United States history, new legislation was needed to re-establish harmony in the country. The Fourteenth Amendment to the Constitution was ratified on July 9, 1868, and granted citizenship to "all persons born or naturalized in the United States," which included former slaves recently freed. In addition, it forbade states from denying any person "life, liberty or property, without due process of law" or to "deny to any person within its jurisdiction the equal protection of the laws." By directly mentioning the role of the states, the 14th Amendment greatly expanded the protection of civil rights to all Americans and is cited in more litigation than any other amendment. ("Primary Documents in American History") It is important to note that the 14th Amendment was passed as the United States was merging back together after the Civil War. Slaves were freed and given citizenship. Confederate soldiers, politicians, and supporters were an issue. In fact, President Andrew Johnson did not proclaim an end of the hostilities of the Civil War until a few months after the passing of the 14th Amendment. The greatest challenge facing the United States Congress after the war was how to "close the war" and prevent another from happening. In order to address these issues there were a few considerations. First being the losses of life and property in the war. The second consideration was the uncertainty about whether the war was really over or was simply in reprise at the time the Congress met. The third and most important consideration was the task of economic and political reconstruction to try to put the country back together again. (42 Akron) Also needed in the Constitution was better clarification on what exactly it meant to be a citizen. The14th Amendment would link citizenship to certain rights that citizens would hold that could not be infringed upon by any level of government. The 14th Amendment would make a sort of social compact, stating that in exchange for allegiance to the federal government by a citizen, the citizen would receive protection for the guarantee of basic fundamental rights outlined in the Constitution. (Farber, 1994)

The 14th Amendment to the Constitution was introduced by the post-Civil War Republicans as a way to not grant new rights, but to instead give the federal government clarification to enforce the Bill of Rights. The Republican Party at that time was closely aligned with the ideology of natural law and the theories and writings of John Locke, whose writings were influential in the development of America and a valuable source to the Founding Fathers. Seeing themselves as protectors of the original American thought and not wanting to create new thoughts, aligning with Locke's ideals was the method chosen to bring the country back to the way it was originally formed in regards to human rights. Locke's Second Treatise has a discussion in which it describes that a man in nature lives under no governmental law, but still adheres to a natural law. Among this natural law is the right to freedom and to any property created by his own labors. All men are equal in this right to have natural freedom. The theory of natural laws would have appealed to the Republicans at the time due to the frontier nature of most of the relatively young United States. (Farber, 1994)

The government guarantees the protection of a citizen's basic rights outlined in the Bill of Rights, but how does one decide what is the correct application of the law or right? This usually falls to the courts who refer to previous cases in history, but early on William Blackstone's Commentaries on the Laws of England were used. Blackstone provided information and background for a variety of issues, including the practical dynamics of freedom of speech and the criminal prosecution of the free speaker if shown to influence another to break the law. Blackstone held plainly that it is a legitimate goal of a country to punish "any dangerous or offensive writings, which, when published . . . be adjudged of a pernicious tendency . . . to preserve the 'peace and good order." Blackstone's views were used by the Founding Fathers when faced with war and also by President Lincoln when faced with the burden of fighting his own country to make the country whole again. (Errickson, "Lincoln's First Amendment Record")

Chapter 2

Suppression of Constitutional Rights

Suppressing personal freedoms that are granted in the Constitution by the national government is nothing new when national security is threatened. In fact, this suppression of constitutional freedoms began almost as soon as the Constitution was ratified. In 1798 the Alien and Sedition Acts were passed as war with France seemed likely. These acts allowed for the deportation and detention of non-citizens and prohibited malicious writings against the government. James Madison and a few others were furious at this infraction on citizens' rights, and fought to have it repealed within two years. In 1861 President Abraham Lincoln suspended habeas corpus and called for the arrest of all dissidents. This suspension was also used to detain influential citizens and lawmakers sympathetic to the Confederate states to prevent states from succeeding from the Union. In 1863 the Habeas Corpus Act was passed that allowed President Lincoln to free or detain prisoners at his will without trial or impunity for the duration of the Civil War. During the 1917-1918 World War I years, the Espionage and Sedition Act was imposed that allowed for severe penalties for any speech, statement, or article that was written against or interfered with the government during wartime. Labor union leader Eugene V.

Debs was sentenced to 10 years in prison for giving an antiwar speech as a result of this act. The attack at Pearl Harbor in December of 1941 by the Japanese Empire prompted United States President Franklin Delano Roosevelt to authorize the relocation and interment of more than 120,000 Japanese-Americans in camps for the duration of the war. In 1947 President Harry S. Truman established the Federal Employee Loyalty Program, which required all government employees to sign loyalty oaths and submit to loyalty investigations. (Calabresi, 2013)

Chapter 3

9/11 Attacks

The sleeping giant was awakened once again with the first major attack against the United States since the Japanese bombed Pearl Harbor in 1941. On September 11, 2001 at 8:46 a.m. American Airline flight 11, which was a Boeing 767 struck the north tower of the World Trade Center. At 9:03 a.m. a second aircraft, United Airlines flight 175, struck the south tower of the World Trade Center. Both towers collapsed within two hours of the impact, causing loss of 2,800 lives including 403 emergency personnel who were on the scene. Financial losses are estimated at $33-36 billion according to the Federal Reserve Bank. (Proyor, J. P. 2009) The planes were hijacked by Islamic terrorists from Saudi Arabia and other Arab nations. Financing the ordeal was Osama bin Laden and his al-Qaeda organization. Motivation for the attack was the disapproval of the United States support of Israel, its involvement in the Persian Gulf War, and its continued military presence in the Middle East. Some of the terrorists were reported to have taken flying lessons in the United States and had lived in the U.S. for over a year. The terrorists were reported to have taken over the planes with box cutters and knives that were smuggled through security. At 9 p.m., President George W. Bush delivered a televised address from the Oval Office, declaring, "Terrorist attacks can shake the foundations of our biggest buildings, but they cannot touch the foundation of America. These acts shatter steel, but they cannot dent the steel of American resolve." In a reference to the eventual U.S. military response he declared, "We will make no distinction between the terrorists who committed these acts and those who harbor them." This attack led to Operation Enduring Freedom, the international effort to end the Taliban regime in Afghanistan and destroy Osama bin Laden's terrorist network based there. U.S. forces had effectively removed the Taliban from operational power within two months, but the war continued in Pakistan as the military continued to fight insurgent Taliban. On May 2, 2011, almost 10 years after the World Trade Center attack, Osama bin Laden was finally tracked down and killed by U.S. forces at a hideout in Abbottabad, Pakistan. In June 2011, President Barack Obama announced the beginning of large-scale troop withdrawals from Afghanistan, with a final withdrawal of U.S. forces tentatively scheduled for 2014. ("9/11 Attacks")

Chapter 4

U.S. Intelligence Community

The World Trade Center attacks on 9/11 demonstrated the intelligence weaknesses and threats that the United States can face in current times. In order to combat this, Congress approved significantly larger intelligence budgets. Congress also passed the most extensive reorganization of the intelligence community since post World War II. The Intelligence Reform and Terrorism Prevention Act of 2004 created a Director of National Intelligence with specific job duties: 1.) head the intelligence community 2.) serve as the principal intelligence adviser to the President, and 3.) oversee and direct the acquisition of major collections systems. This position would concentrate on the intelligence community in its entirety.

The intelligence community consists of the following:

Central Intelligence Agency (CIA)

Bureau of Intelligence and Research, Department of State (INR)

Defense Intelligence Agency (DIA)

National Security Agency (NSA)

National Reconnaissance Office (NRO)

National Geospatial-Intelligence Agency (NGA)

Federal Bureau of Investigation (FBI)

Army Intelligence

Navy Intelligence

Air Force Intelligence

Marine Corps Intelligence

Department of Homeland Security (DHS)

Coast Guard (CG)

Treasury Department

Energy Department

Drug Enforcement Administration (DEA)

The CIA is the main component of the intelligence community. All other intelligence offices are components of Cabinet departments with other roles and duties. They participate in intelligence gathering while completing other duties of their departments. The CIA has the task and privilege of being able to cover the whole world. The CIA also collects intelligence with human sources and, on occasion, undertakes covert actions at the direction of the President. (A covert action is an activity or activities of the U.S. government to influence political, economic, or military conditions abroad, where it is intended that the U.S. role will not be apparent or acknowledged publicly.) The Department of Defense (DOD) has three offices that also collect intelligence—the National Security Agency (NSA), the National Reconnaissance Office (NRO), and the National Geospatial-Intelligence Agency (NGA). NSA is responsible for signals intelligence and has collection sites throughout the world. The NRO develops and operates reconnaissance satellites. The NGA prepares the geospatial data—ranging from maps and charts to sophisticated computerized databases—necessary for humanitarian operations and for targeting in an era in which military operations are dependent upon precision-guided weapons. In addition to these three agencies, the Defense Intelligence Agency (DIA) is responsible for providing DOD with analytical products. The key intelligence functions of the FBI relate to counter-terrorism and counter-intelligence. Since September of 2001, the counter-intelligence function has grown to immense importance. The FBI went under a thorough re-organization and has added many agents and analysts to its staff. As part of the re-organization, the FBI is expected to to coordinate with all other law enforcement in any counter-intelligence or counter-terrorism activities. The Homeland Security Act provided the new Department of Homeland Security (DHS) responsibilities for fusing law enforcement and intelligence information relating to terrorist threats to the homeland. The Office of Intelligence and Analysis in DHS participates in the inter-agency counter-terrorism efforts and, along with the FBI, has focused on ensuring that state and local law enforcement are communicated with. The Coast Guard, now part of DHS, deals with information relating to maritime security and homeland defense. The Energy Department analyzes foreign nuclear weapons programs as well as nuclear nonproliferation and energy-security issues. It also has a robust counterintelligence effort. The

Treasury Department collects and processes information that may affect U.S. fiscal and monetary policies. Treasury also covers the issue of terrorist financing. (Best Jr, R. A. 2011)

Also in response to the 9/11 attacks, Congress passed the USA Patriot Act in 2001 which gave law-enforcement powers to search without warrants, eavesdrop, and detain and deport terrorism suspects. In 2011 President Barack Obama gave federal agents new powers to data-mine terrorism suspects' devices and communications and delay the reading of Miranda rights to suspects under arrest as well as new surveillance powers and the right to interview witnesses without identifying themselves as FBI agents. (Calabresi, 2013)

The Patriot Act broadly expands the definition of terrorism, meaning many non-violent social groups could meet the definition of a terrorist, and not be allowed 1st Amendment protection of freedom of speech. If a librarian or records clerk told a suspect that law enforcement was investigating them, the librarian could be prosecuted for the offense and not be protected under the 1st amendment. The right of freedom of association is diminished as law enforcement can infiltrate any group it wants to to spy on what essentially could be law-abiding organizations and religious groups. A person can become a target of investigation just for being associated with a particular group. Fourth amendment rights to unlawful search and seizure are now diminished as law enforcement essentially only has to claim that anything is part of a terrorist investigation and no Judicial oversight or permission is required. The 14th amendment provides for equal protection, but 82,000 men from Arab, Muslim, and South Asian countries were required to register under a special registration program brought about to combat terrorism. Over 13,000 are now in deportation hearings despite never having been charged with any terrorist activities. ("Eroding Liberty")

An issue with the constitutional rights of the "people of the United States" is what exactly is meant by "the people". Are the references to "the people" meant to target particular individuals or official American citizens? Are "the people of the United States" everyone in the country regardless of the status of official citizenship? Also, does "the people" mean different things in different amendments? The Supreme Court has had to tackle these questions in the past few decades. The 1990 United States vs. Verdugo-Urquidez decision states that "the people" refers to "those people who are part of a national community" or who have "substantial connections" to the United States. The key to this decision is not citizenship, but the extent of one's connection with the United States. The court also went on to state that this definition of "the people" applied consistently throughout the Bill of Rights. In the 2008 case of District of Columbia vs. Heller, the court quoted the Verdugo-Urquidez decision and once again suggested that the phrase "the people" had consistent meaning throughout the Constitution. Heller also said that "the people" refers to all members of a political community. The reference to "all members of a political community" made this decision controversial because that itself requires some interpretation, which has led to other cases and other decisions. Does the reference to "all members of a political community" refer to only registered voters? If so, this would exclude many individuals in the United States from protection under Constitution. ("The meaning," 2013)

After 9/11 and through the newly made and re-organized offices, the United States government started many activities that are seen by some as infringements of civil liberties protected by the Constitution. Under established Supreme Court findings, however, it is important to note that a person has no legally recognized expectation of privacy in any information given to a third party. So, therefore, any information collected from a third party does not constitute a "search" that is protected by the Fourth Amendment. The Supreme Court states that the Constitution does not apply to foreigners outside of the United States. Also, the Supreme Court States that the reasonableness of a "warrant-less search" depends on the balance of the person's fourth amendment rights against the promotion of legitimate governmental business. (Litt, 2013)

So what exactly is the government collecting? According to a source from the Office of the Director of National Intelligence, the government is mostly collecting metadata. Metadata, the information about communications, is less intrusive to the target and can narrow down who should be investigated further. The Office of the Director of National Intelligence says it is simply not true that the government is listening to every word said by every citizen and reading all e-mails and text messages. The government is collecting metadata under the assumption that this data is given to a third party and is therefore exempt from the protection provided under the fourth amendment. (Litt, 2013)

Chapter 5

Fear

Fear is the main emotion used to get the American public to buy into the suppression of constitutional rights. Americans want more homeland security than they need because they are afraid of terrorists[1]. Information about terrorism comes mostly from politicians and government organizations with their own agendas and interests. Unfortunately, members from all political affiliations and politicians from many offices are using this scare tactic. The information given to the press to release to the population can create political demand for counter-terrorism policies. These policies can limit freedoms and usually also have unrelated issues lumped in as a way to get issues passed without question. By exploiting the public's fear of terrorism, governments can justify spending and wars that are being fought for other reasons. Tell an American citizen that we are going to war to spread democracy to a dictator state and he may be hesitant to spend money and risk lives, but tell him we are going to fight the terrorist who bombed a building that killed innocent Americans, and suddenly he is on board. The main objective of spreading democracy was still done, but using fear of terrorism allowed it to happen by gaining support of the citizen. Terrorism is

---

[1] The chances of an American dying in a terrorist attack in the United States is 1 in 20 million. (How Scared..)

not about the violence but about the emotion it provokes. Terrorism is an act done to mainly gain attention--sure, lives and property are lost, but terrorism is all about the publicity. Humans are emotional creatures and easily overreact to terrorism. What needs to happen is for politicians to be honest with citizens about the threat. Also, citizens need to learn to do independent research and question the motivation of politicians and the government in general. (Friedman, 2011)

Even though Americans are fearful of terrorism, they are more fearful of losing civil liberties. A recent gallop poll reports that 71 percent of Americans are not agreeable on giving up civil liberties in exchange for protection against terrorism[2]. Even people in law enforcement are learning that befriending and respecting the different groups in the United States is the best way to thwart terrorism. Terrorism comes from the radicals inside various groups, and having partners inside the groups come forward with information is a far better solution than alienating the groups and making them all feel that they are under investigation. This approach also does not infringe on any particular constitutional rights of the people involved. It is simply not feasible to investigate every radical in the United States. It is important to remember that the Founding Fathers of the United States were "radicals", so the Constitution was written to somewhat protect individual rights to be a radical. It is somewhat naive to think that the government can stop every school shooter and every person with violent ideologies and knowledge of explosives. (Calabresi, 2013)

---

[2] 49% of citizens were agreeable on giving up personal freedoms in 2002 when the 9/11 attacks were fresh in the minds of citizens and publicized daily in the media. (Civil Liberties)

The modern world we live in is a fragile one. Technology improvements over the last 200 years have made the lives of Americans much easier, and shifted the country from its agrarian roots to mostly a city-based industrial and business focused economy. As the populations of cities rise, they become targets for the few radical terrorists with a mission to get the most attention for their efforts. When James Madison and the founding fathers penned the constitution and the Bill of Rights, they wanted to create a basis for the United States to prosper forever, and knowing that the country would evolve, the wording was made specific yet broad enough so it could be interpreted for the times and still be relevant today and 200 years from now. Individual freedoms for all citizens of the United States were the foundation that the Constitution was built on, and citizens need to ensure they keep the freedoms allowed to us. While a law-abiding citizen probably wouldn't notice or care that his communication is being monitored, one should ask what is happening to that information and can it be used for something detrimental later. There are many occurrences in world history where a seemingly minor infraction has led to major turmoil. There is a delicate balancing act when it comes individual rights or freedoms and national security. Current political party platforms from both the Republican and Democratic parties say they want the government to be open and transparent and to safeguard constitutional rights. But politicians from both parties continue to pass legislation that does the opposite. Unscrupulous politicians will exploit emotion and feelings about terrorism and suppression of individual freedoms to further their own agendas and personal gain. The constitutional system has checks and balances in place, and as a citizen one has to participate and question the government to ensure that the best interests of the country and its people are being upheld. James madison said, "All men having power ought to be distrusted to a certain degree." Being an informed citizen, questioning motives, and participating in government is an honorable way to put the distrust to use.

References

"9/11 Attacks." History.com. A&E Television Networks, n.d. Web. 4 June 2014. <http://www.history.com/topics/9-11-attacks>.

42 Akron L. Rev. 1019. Retrieved from
    www.lexisnexis.com/hottopics/lnacademic

Best Jr, R. A. (2011). Intelligence Issues for Congress. *Congressional Research Service: Report*, 1-29.

Bill of Rights. (n.d.). *Bill of Rights Institute Bill of Rights Comments*. Retrieved June 1, 2014, from http://billofrightsinstitute.org/founding-documents/bill-of-rights/

Calabresi, M. M. A. z. A. M. S. (2013). Homeland Insecurity. *Time, 181*(18), 22.

Civil Liberties. (n.d.). *Gallup.Com*. Retrieved June 10, 2014, from

    http://www.gallup.com/poll/5263/civil-liberties.aspx

Constitution of the United States. (2013).   Columbia Electronic Encyclopedia, 6th Edition, 1-3.
Eroding Liberty. (n.d.). *Rights and Freedoms lost since 9-11*. Retrieved June 9, 2014, from http://www.nyclu.org/pdfs/eroding_liberty.pdf

Errickson, Eve. "Lincoln's First Amendment Record." Lincoln's First Amendment Record. N.p., n.d. Web. 9 June 2014. <http://lincolncottage.org/HabeasCorpus-EveErrickson.pdf>.

Farber, Daniel A. and Muench, John E. , Ideological Origins of the Fourteenth Amendment, 1 Const. Comment. 235 (1994), Available at: http://scholarship.law.berkeley.edu/facpubs/394

Friedman, B. H. (2011). Managing Fear: The Politics of Homeland Security (Vol. 126, pp. 77): Academy of Political Science.

How Scared of Terrorism Should You Be?. (n.d.). *Reason.com*.

Retrieved June 18, 2014, from

http://reason.com/archives/2011/09/06/how-scared-of-

terrorism-should

Litt, R. S. (2013a). Privacy, Technology and National Security (Vol. 79, pp. 313-321): McMurry Inc.

Miller Center. (n.d.). *American President: James Madison: Life Before the Presidency*. Retrieved June 5, 2014, from http://millercenter.org/president/madison/essays/biography/2

Primary Documents in American History. (n.d.). *14th Amendment to the U.S. Constitution: Primary Documents of American History (Virtual Programs & Services, Library of Congress)*. Retrieved May 31, 2014, from

http://www.loc.gov/rr/program/bib/ourdocs/14thamendment.

html

Proyor, J. P. (2009). The 2001 World Trade Center disaster:

summary and evaluation of experiences. *European Journal of Trauma & Emergency Surgery, 35*(3), 212-224.

The Meaning of "The People" In The Constitution. (2013).
Harvard Law Review,   126(4), 1078-1099.